MW01491210

Talitha Koum:

Little Girl I Say To You, Get Up!

Stephanie C. Lewis

Speaking engagements and bookings:

Stephanie C. Lewis, Founder,

Heart of a Princess Enterprise-

heartofaprincessenterprise@gmail.com

DEDICATION

* * * * ● ● ● * * * *

I wish to personally thank the following people for your love, prayers, support, and inspiration as I pursue the vision for this book that God placed within me. There are so many who, without you, this would not have been possible. I can't name you all but please know that you have not gone unnoticed.

A special thank you to:

Joann Rosario Condrey

Rainfire Church Maranatha

The Write Media Group, LLC

All of my family, sisters, and friends in Christ

A special thank you is in order to my loving husband. You have always been my supporter, challenger, encourager, and biggest fan. I thank you for that.

Contents

STEPHANIE C. LEWIS

INTRODUCTION

* * * * ● ● ● * * * *

Faith is the confidence that what we hope for will actually happen. It gives us assurance about things we cannot see (Hebrews 11:1, NLT). The funny thing about that is having faith and hope alone won't make it magically happen. You are going to have to put in some work, too. James 2:26, states that faith without works is dead. Well honey, if the Bible stating it isn't enough for you to believe, let me see if I can help. In 2010, I was given the task of writing a book. Five years later, I still had faith I would write the book. But not one ounce of work was put into writing, the book and I still wasn't an author! The closest I came to putting in work was asking God to tell me what to write.

Well here it is. I finally wrote my book, but it took more than just having faith that it would happen. I had to start writing. As I began my journey as an author, God began to give me words to write. So what's my point? It's that it is now time to put in work for that raise, new job, home, husband, or whatever it is you desire. It's not just going to fall into your lap. Faith = Prayer + Work.

In Mark 5:41, Jesus goes to heal a little girl and He says to her "Talitha Koum." It means, "Little girl, I say to you get up!" Well I'm not Jesus, but I think it's ok for me to say the same thing to you. *Talitha Koum* Little girl (woman), it's time to Get Up! Get up and start making moves towards that goal you have. I hope this book inspires you and pushes you to start that new journey of

work to go with your faith. So let's get to work!

Day 1: Get Up!

He took her by the hand and said to her, *"Talitha koum!" (which means "Little girl, I say to you, get up!") - Mark 5:41*

As I mentioned in the introduction, Faith=Prayer +Work. I want to add to that equation for today. Faith +Prayer +Work = Purpose. When you activate your faith, which happens through prayer and work, then you start to achieve your true calling in life. God created each of us for a purpose and each person on this earth was created for a specific reason. There are some who know their purpose early in life and there are others who take a while to figure it out. Regardless of which category you fit into, eventually you figure it out. At that point, it's time to move.

Side note: If you haven't figured it out yet, then it's time to go back and focus on the prayer part of our earlier equation.

Let's take a look at the story of the little girl in Mark. She appeared to be dead. Her family, friends, and spectators were mourning her when Jesus arrived. Everything about her situation looked dead. Jesus, however, saw more. He saw life! He questioned the crowd and told them that she wasn't dead but asleep. They wavered in their faith, the same way we do at times because of how the situation appears, but Jesus saw something else. He put everyone out who did not believe and he said to the little girl, "Talitha Koum!" The scripture says that she immediately got up and started walking. My interpretation of that is as soon as she heard the voice of the Lord telling her what to do, she acted on it. She started walking, which meant that she had a purpose. She knew her direction and she believed that her situation was not dead.

I would like to encourage everyone reading this book to follow the example of the little girl. When you hear the voice of the Lord telling you to do something, it's time to immediately get moving. Just as Jesus did, it is important to remove anything and anyone who doesn't believe in your purpose. Focus on the voice of the Lord and start moving. Jesus only allowed those who believed to remain in the room while He spoke to the little girl, and when she rose and walked, everyone was amazed. You need to do the same: Only allow those who believe in you and your purpose to stick around.

Keep close to those that will pray for you, encourage you, keep you accounted for, and you will rise.

I am always amazed at the fact that as soon as she rose, she walked around. To me that means she knew there was no time to waste. She knew that because Jesus told her what to do, she needed to do her part and allow Him to take care of the rest. After she rose, Jesus told her family to give her something to eat. That part just makes me love Jesus even more (if that's even possible). It confirms to me, and hopefully it will for you as well, that as long as you do what He has commanded, He will make provision for everything that you need to continue the journey towards your purpose. He already knows everything that is needed for you to be successful. The scripture doesn't say that the little girl told Jesus she was hungry; it says she walked. Jesus already knew and as she was walking, he was providing.

That gives me so much hope for everything I've set out to accomplish. I know that as God continues to reveal my purpose to me, He will also make sure that everything I need is already handled even before I realize I need it. Today, I want to encourage you to focus on doing your part. Listen to God, let Him direct you and you take the first step. He already knows what you need and He knows when He supplies it, all you have to do is get up and walk! Take a walk today! You will be amazed at how far you can travel with Jesus as your guide.

Day 2: You are Set Apart

• • • • ● ● ● • • • •

Before I formed you in the womb, I knew you. Before you were born I set you apart, I appointed you as a prophet to the nations.
-Jeremiah 1:5

Today I want you to remember that you are different. You are set apart; you are not like the rest. Isn't that great!? Who wants to be ordinary, plain, or usual? No one. You don't want to be that way and God doesn't want that for you either. We talked about this a little yesterday, but let me just remind you that you were born with a distinct purpose. God says so in Jeremiah 1:5. He says that he set you apart even before you were born. So if you feel different, look different, act different, it's all part of God's plan for you. He wants you to be different and stand out so that people are drawn to you because of those differences. God ultimately gets the glory because there is "something different" about you that will make others want to know more about how you got that way.

As a woman, I can attest to the fact that it is hard to be different. Society creates an image whether it's size, height, personality, skin tone, hair color, hair texture, occupation, philosophy and other distinctions that are used as an example of "normal." The problem is that unintentionally we all find ourselves trying to either live up to that standard or gravitate towards that standard. Every year there is a list that is distributed of the 50 most beautiful women in the world and these women are beautiful, yes, but they may not look like you or me.

When that happens, those who don't look "beautiful" by the world's definitely, start to feel less than adequate. That's why you find people taking drastic measures such as cosmetic surgery, and other extreme alterations. These people want to look like the standard that's been set by others. When that standard still isn't achieved, we compensate in other ways because now there is a self-esteem issue.

God created us all and the Bible says that we are created in his image. He determined everything about us before we were even born, so we have to be disciplined enough to hold on to that idea and be confident and sure of who we are. Having this confidence means that there is no more settling; no more accepting anything less than what you are truly deserving of. More than any other love or acceptance that we seek, God loves us and accepts us the most. We all should have confidence in that because directly linked to our purpose is the task of representing Him.

Today I want to remind you to be confident in who you are and who God has called you to be. He said that He appointed us as prophets to the nation. That means that we are His spokespeople. We are direct reflections of God and there is nothing more beautiful than the image and love of God. I challenge you to make the bold declaration that you are set apart and have no desire to be anything other than what God has called you to be. You have no desire to have anything or anyone other than what has been ordained by God.

Throughout these 30 days, we will condition ourselves to communicate with God more. Doing so will help us make better decisions about everything in life.

Today understand that it's ok to be different. You were made that way on purpose.

Day 3: Attitude and Behavior

●　●　●　●　●　●　●　●　●　●　●

Whatever happens, conduct yourselves in a manner worthy of the gospel of Christ. Then, whether I come and see you or only hear about you in my absence, I will know that you stand firm in the one Spirit,[a] striving together as one for the faith of the gospel.
-Philippians 1:27
In your relationships with one another, have the same mindset as Christ Jesus: -Philippians 2:5

Have you ever been so upset about something that you wanted to immediately respond with your first reaction? You know what I mean, have you ever been so upset that you wanted to curse, fight, and just say harsh things to the person who upset you? Maybe you have been out with friends who aren't carrying themselves in the best manner and you are tempted to behave or carry yourself the same way, even though that's not your personality. Have you ever had a bad day? On that day doesn't it seem as though everyone wants to talk to you or worse—annoy you?

How do you handle all of these situations? Do you go ahead and use the most creative forms of profanity that you can find? Do you fight the person who cut in front of you on the highway? Do you have a bad attitude with every coworker you encounter at work simply because you are having a bad day? Do you walk around with a negative attitude despite the many blessings that God has bestowed in your life? The answer to all of these questions should be no. As children of God, we are expected to carry ourselves a certain way. That doesn't mean that we won't be tempted to react the way I mentioned earlier, but through Jesus Christ, we are to have the discipline or self-control to carry ourselves in a way that is pleasing to God.

Today we will take a look at two scriptures. Both are extremely important and provide great insight into the way that God expects us to behave. In the first scripture, Paul says that whatever happens, conduct yourself in a manner worthy of the Gospel of Christ. I like that he says "whatever" because that means no matter the situation, no matter how upset we become, no matter how badly we feel, no matter how antagonized we are, we are to conduct ourselves in a way that reflects Christ. Remember, we are disciples—followers of Christ—and as disciples, we are Christ's ambassadors. We are representing Him. Our actions should make others want to know the Christ we serve.

That means we have to make sure we are a reflection of Christ in every situation.

The second scripture says our attitude should be the same as that of Christ Jesus. Now trust me, I understand that those are very big shoes to fill, but as followers of Christ, we should strive to live the life that Jesus led. The great thing about that is Jesus is right there with us to help us and guide us daily. When we are weak, He is strong; we are angry, He can calm us. Remember today bring Christ along with you in everything you do. Incorporating Him into your life will give you a peace that is unexplainable even in the midst of the worst chaos.

Today let's all strive to live like Jesus!

Day 4: Treasures of Truth

• • • • • ● • • • • •

Do not conform to the pattern of this world, but be transformed

by the renewing of your mind. -Romans 12:2

Today's scripture reminds us to keep our minds clear from the clutter that this world can create. I think that we all can agree that there is a lot happening in this world, in our lives, and in our minds. Collectively we are exposed to more and have more of a variety of methods to expose us to more than at any other time in our history. Our eyes see and our ears hear more now than ever before. With all of the different methods of communication available (television, phones, radio, tablets, computers, etc.) we are surrounded by access to a variety of cultures, beliefs, lifestyles, and habits that have the power to influence our own ideals.

Think about it for a moment. Why do you want some of the things that you want? Is it because you saw someone else with it? Why do you dress the way you dress? Is it because your favorite celebrity has that style? Are you interested in a certain car, house, shoe, or lifestyle because it is popular? Are you modeling your lifestyle after your favorite celebrity because you can now follow them on social media? Do you watch certain shows and now find yourself intrigued by the subject matter that you see each week when otherwise you would have never given it a second thought? Everything we do is influenced in some way, but today I want to remind you to keep your mind focused on the greatest influence there is; and that is Christ.

Today's scripture speaks to this very idea by reminding us that no matter what we are exposed to, we must constantly keep our mind focused on our foundation: Christ.

Let's face it, we all have guilty pleasures and we all have certain weaknesses that have the potential to shake our foundation. But we cannot conform to those weaknesses. We cannot conform to those things that are popular if they go against the very principles set forth by the Word of God. The images of beauty that are suggested within the media, the images of relationships that we see on reality shows, the ideas that we have about other races, cultures, and ethnicities that we see on the news are all forces that have the potential to contradict what we truly believe. When the scripture says, "do not conform" it is very clear that there will be an influx of potential threats that could shake your foundation, that didn't surprise God and it shouldn't surprise you. The scripture also tells us to be transformed by the renewing of our minds. That means the most effective way to stay true to ourselves is through constant affirmation with the daily renewal of our minds.

How do we do this you ask? By focusing on everything that the Word of God has spoken to us.

If you start to feel unattractive or unworthy, renew your mind with Psalm 139:14 that says, "I praise you because I am fearfully and wonderfully made." If you feel desperate or unsure of your future, remember Matthew 6:33 that says to "seek ye first his Kingdom and his righteousness and all these things will be given to you as well." When you feel afraid, remember Psalm 23:4 that says "yea though I walk through the valley of the shadow of death, I will fear no evil for you are with me." My point is that renewing your mind falls in line with studying and understanding what God says about you. Ultimately renewing your mind means you will *change* the way that you think. In order to truly see a difference in your life, you must practice a more positive way of thinking. Change is only change when you've changed. I challenge you to begin the practice of changing the way you think, today!

Day 5: Stay Away from Anger

• • • • ● ● ● • • • •

Fools give full vent to their rage, but the wise bring calm in the end.

-Proverbs 29:11

Today let's focus on staying calm in the midst of intense situations. The scripture very candidly points out that those who succumb to their feelings of anger and rage are like fools, but those who are wise find calm in their situations. How many times have your succumbed to your anger? Did someone say something to you that sent you over the top; or perhaps someone cut you off on the road and sent you into a fit of rage? Do your children, spouse, or coworkers say and do things that bring about uncontrollable anger? I am confident that at times we have all given in to our anger, but the Bible encourages us to find ways to subdue that anger.

I am so glad that yesterday we discussed renewing our minds because today is the perfect opportunity to practice that idea. When situations become intense, try renewing your mind with thoughts of peace and meditation. Throughout the Bible there is scripture that supports the idea of finding calm and peace in the midst of trial. Let's take a look and when you have time, study and meditate on these scriptures to really understand their value:

- Proverbs 20:3 – It is to one's honor to avoid strife, but every fool is quick to quarrel.

- Proverbs 19:11 – A person's wisdom yields patience; it is to one's glory to overlook an offense.

- Proverbs 17:14 – Starting a quarrel is like breaching a dam, so drop the matter before a dispute breaks out.

- Proverbs 14:30 – A heart at peace gives life to the body, but envy rots the bones.

Yes, I know I gave you a lot of scriptures to study, but that's because anger is one of our biggest and sometimes most uncontrollable weaknesses. It takes a little extra effort and discipline to really get a grip on how we handle our anger.

Notice that the main idea of each scripture is that those who give in to their anger are perceived in a more negative way than those who diffuse or avoid the confrontation. Those who are peaceful are associated with wisdom and poise. Which way do you want to be perceived? Are you the one who creates chaos and havoc or are you the wiser counsel who seeks a peaceful resolution?

I would like to encourage you to be the latter. Peace and serenity cause a person way more good than the harmful effects of those who constantly create chaos. The next time you feel the need to display anger and rage, remember Psalm 23:5, "You prepare a table before me in the presence of my enemies. You anoint my head with oil; my cup overflows."

That means you should not worry about your enemies or those who are against you because God will vindicate you. He will anoint you and bless you tremendously. Just trust him.

Today practice taking on the characteristics of Jesus, and extend grace, mercy, and peace to your enemies and adversaries.

Day 6: The Tongue:
The Problem Child!

* • • • • ● ● • • • •

My dear brothers, take note of this: Everyone should be quick to listen, slow to speak, and slow to become angry, for man's anger does not bring about the righteous life that God desires. -James 1:19-20

If anyone considers himself religious and yet does not keep a tight rein on his tongue, He deceives himself and his religion is worthless. -James 1:26

I can almost hear your thoughts to me right now. You are thinking, "Didn't we just talk about anger and controlling the tongue? Why are we still here? Why do we have two scriptures today?"

I totally understand your questions because when God gave me these scriptures and today's topic, I thought the exact same thing. The answer is this: although the scripture does speak on anger, the focus for today is mainly on controlling the tongue. You may be thinking these two concepts are the same, but although the two (anger and self-control) do go hand in hand, we will dig a little deeper into controlling what we say at *all* times, not just when we are angry.

Have you ever had a conversation with a person and they are telling you all of the things you have done to upset them or hurt their feelings? Have you ever had someone tell you they need to talk to you about their problems and as you are listening to them, you are already thinking about how you are going to respond to what they are saying? Have you ever reached out to someone for a listening ear only to barely get a word in because they were so quick to provide their insight into your issue? All of these scenarios are perfect examples of a person's inability to be slow to speak.

Today's scriptures are very specific about the importance of holding your tongue and thinking before you speak. There are many consequences that evolve from not adhering to these instructions. The first piece of guidance provided in this scripture is that we should be quick to listen. There is such an added value in listening. When you really take the time to listen to what a person is saying—not just with their words but with their eyes, body language and their heart—you can learn so much more than a two-hour debate could ever provide. Listening, observing, and thinking, are four key ways to avoid unnecessary conflict and miscommunication.

I never have meaningful conversation over a text message or email, simply because I am not able to truly get to the core of the other person's feelings, sincerity, or intentions. I can't look into their eyes and hear their voice. I can't truly understand the origin of their comments, because I am not able to listen to them.

Many times we listen by simply being silent until it's our turn to speak. That's not effective communication. Doing this is a guaranteed way to miss the important points of what a person is saying to you and responding from an emotional, un-thoughtful perspective that results in miscommunication, anger, and conflict. Listening helps us to really understand the content and even if by chance the intentions of the other party are not positive, being slow to speak will help you develop a rational, calm response. After all, as

Christians we are representatives of Christ in our everyday actions and deeds.

Today I encourage you to begin a habit of being slow to speak by listening and then thinking clearly before responding. Also consider that sometimes the best response is no response; instead, pray and ask God for self-control, wisdom, and patience in all of your daily interactions. It is a process, but as with any exercise, you will get stronger through repetition.

Day 7: Unashamed

I eagerly expect and hope that I will in no way be ashamed, but will have sufficient courage so that now as always, Christ will be exalted in my body, whether by life or by death. -Philippians 1:20

Was there ever a time that you felt ashamed of something or someone? Have you ever gone to an event with a person and felt totally ashamed to introduce them to others? I'm sure that many teenagers throughout history can attest to being ashamed to have their parents eat with them during their school lunch period or chaperone their senior prom. Have you ever thought about why that may be? I'm guessing it could be because of the fear of how people will respond or the type of attention that those "ashamed moments" will bring.

Now let me ask this question: Can you remember a time that you ever felt that someone was ashamed of you? Maybe they admitted either blatantly or subtly that they were ashamed of the way that you looked, or sounded, or dressed. Many people won't just admit outright to a person that they are ashamed of them, but a person's actions certainly can suggest such. Have you ever had a time in your life when you were ashamed of yourself? Maybe it was the way you looked, spoke, or dressed; or you were hurt and forced to live with a scar or outward symbol of that experience. People who are ashamed are that way for many reasons, whether because of an action or something subconscious. Many times the shame occurs for reasons that no one else even knows about.

Shame is a deep wound whether you are ashamed of yourself or someone else. It is a feeling that is hard to overcome and it takes quite a bit of self-analysis to really strip down to the root cause. My last question to you now is this: Have you ever been ashamed of Christ? Few will ever admit it, but those same subtle actions we discussed earlier that can indicate shame are the same things we do at times unintentionally to Christ.

As Christians, we are mandated to represent Christ in everything we do. There should be something about us that is different from those who are non-believers. That doesn't mean that we should act as though we are better than anyone else, but it means we should represent Him in our actions and deeds. We should behave in a way that makes people curious about why we are the way we are.

Today's scripture encourages us to live a life that boldly represents Christ. That means when everyone else in our circle behaves or reacts in a way that is not Christ-like, we should not be ashamed to continue to do what's right. We should not be ashamed or afraid to talk to others about Christ or even introduce nonbelievers to Christ. We should have courage and the boldness to proclaim that Jesus is our Lord and Savior and we should be willing to share Him and His Word with anyone and everyone.

One thing I have noticed throughout my life is that everything begins and ends with Christ. Having boldness for God and not being afraid to live my life for Him actually helps me to live boldly through my own insecurities. As I strengthen my relationship with Christ, I also learn how to strengthen my earthly relationships. It is amazing to me that the answer to everything is simple: Christ.

Today I want us to focus on living courageously for Christ. In doing so we become less insecure about ourselves, we become more in tune with our sense of purpose and we learn to embrace the person that God has created us to be. Today step outside of your comfort zone and demonstrate that you belong to Christ in some way, whether an act of kindness, an opportunity to minister to someone who doesn't know Him, or any other expression of love. Something in your actions and deeds will be so magnetic to people that they will notice the Jesus in you and in return, He will receive the glory. What an amazing way to show God that we are unashamed and living boldly and courageously for Him in all that we do.

Day 8: You Are Forgiven

So Embrace It!

• • • • ● ● ● • • • •

But you are a chosen people, a royal priesthood, a holy nation,
God's special possession, that you may declare the praises of him who
called you out of darkness into his wonderful light. -1 Peter 2:9

The great thing about Jesus is that He died for us!
All that He endured throughout His journey to the cross
was for you and me. The sacrifice that was made for us
was so that we could have forgiveness for our sins and
live our eternal life with God.   It is so important to
remember that *Christ died for you.* He knew that you
would do what you did long before you were even born,
but He died so that you could be redeemed. Now I

understand that people will hold your shortcomings against you until the end of time, but always remember that God is no man. Redemption, deliverance, forgiveness and repentance are available to you and once you accept it, you can't give it back.

I don't want to sound too deep here, but the truth is once God has forgiven you of your sins, that's it. The only stipulation is that you must know Christ and sincerely accept Him as your Lord and Savior. If you do, then the next step is to strive daily to live for Him. There will be days when you fall; we all do, but the wonderful thing about our Savior is when you fall, you can repent and all is forgiven. Not only are you forgiven, but Christ can also help you to improve as you continue on your journey.

Have you ever heard of the term Double Jeopardy? It's basically a legal term that means that a person can't get a second prosecution for an offense for which they have already been acquitted or convicted. The great thing about *your* case is that because of Jesus' sacrifice, you won't be convicted and what's even better is you won't ever be prosecuted for that offense again. This can be a tough concept to accept because people will always try to reconvict you for your past.

No matter how far in the past the offense may have occurred, or what you have done to redeem yourself, people won't always be as forgiving as Christ. What often happens is that because people don't forgive us, we in turn don't forgive ourselves. When others constantly give us a second, third, or even fourth prosecution, we tend to do the same. We also have a pretty bad habit of prosecuting ourselves over and over, but what I want you to remember today is your trial is over and the case was thrown out! You are forgiven. There is no need to dwell on the offense, because God doesn't even see it anymore.

I believe that in addition to eternal life with Him, God allows forgiveness so we can move forward and focus on building a life that's dedicated to Him. God wants you to stop focusing on your past so you can focus on your future with Him. As today's scripture points out, you were specifically chosen, you are royalty and you belong to God. He has a purpose for you and focusing on your shortcomings is only hindering you from moving forward in that purpose. Today, put the past behind you and focus on who God says you are and the plans He has for your life.

Day 9: The Happy Heart

* * * * * ● * * * * *

A happy heart makes the face cheerful, but heartache crushes

the spirit. - Proverbs 15:13

Remember the song by Bobby McFerrin called Don't Worry/Be Happy? To date that song is still in heavy rotation on select radio stations across the country. Although the song is short and pretty simple, the message is clear: If there is less time spent worrying, then that leaves more time to focus on being happy. I know that is easier said than done, but what I also know from my own personal experience is that those words are absolutely true.

I don't know if Mr. McFerrin read this scripture before he wrote that song, but today's scripture is telling us the same thing, "just be happy." I'd like to point out, though, this scripture starts out by referring to "a happy heart." What that says to me is happiness is not *true* happiness unless it resides on the inside of us. The heart is the core of everything vital to life. A healthy heart indicates a healthy body; an unhealthy heart is the gateway to all types of negative health effects and even death. If the Bible is telling us that the heart needs to be happy, then that must mean it is a pretty important characteristic for life.

Now let's be clear and define happiness. I don't think either of us—me or the Bible—are referring to happiness as it pertains to material possessions. In fact, I'm quite confident it means just the opposite. There is a clear contradiction between society's definition of happiness and the Bible's. Happiness as it is referred to here is an inner peace and serenity that is present regardless of any situation or possession. It's a certainty that comes from knowing that through Christ and an eternal life in His kingdom, we have a constant feeling of joy that is present even during our worst hours.

That is true happiness. "Things" can't really make us happy because when the "things" are gone, then they also take our happiness with them. With an inner happiness through Christ; however, we don't worry about the temporary happiness of the world. We know that long-standing happiness exists with Christ, who will never leave us and controls all things.

The last point I would like to make is I don't think it is a coincidence that this scripture emphasizes a happy heart and the very foundation of our relationship with Christ begins by accepting Him *in* our hearts. Remember the key to salvation is that we believe in our hearts that Christ died for us and was raised from the dead (Romans 10:9). What I conclude from that is where Christ resides, so does our happiness.

Today before you focus on happiness, let's make sure your heart is filled with Christ. If it's not, I guarantee that by accepting Him as your Lord and Savior you will feel His presence and see a change begin to take place in your life. Soon you will realize the happiness you were searching for was present through Christ the entire time. For those who have already accepted Christ, let's aim to get closer and develop our relationships with Him through increased prayer and communication. I am confident that any happiness we were searching for will show itself as we allow Christ to reveal Himself to us.

Day 10: The Fail-Proof Method

...and my message and my preaching were not in persuasive words of wisdom, but in demonstration of the Spirit and of power, so that your faith would not rest on the wisdom of men, but on the power of God. -2 Corinthians 2:4-5

Today I would like for us to think about trust. Trust is a big commitment and it is also a very vulnerable action. When you trust someone you are putting complete faith in that person. You are trusting that he or she will not hurt or deceive you. If you are in a relationship with someone, you trust that your significant other will not hurt you in any way. In friendships you trust that your friends will honor the intimate conversations and not share them with anyone; you also trust that your friends really are your true friends.

Issues begin when someone betrays your trust. At that point after the trust is broken, it is difficult to reestablish. That's the problem with many relationships, whether dating, marriages, or friendships; once trust is broken it is almost lost. Our society puts a lot of faith and trust in many different things. We trust our physicians, we trust our church leaders, we trust our government leaders, we trust our employers; and we do so to a fault at times because the trust develops into a pedestal. Once that trust is broken, we become crushed, discouraged, and worst of all, distrusting of others. I have gone down this road myself, so I understand the challenge of trusting someone after you have been hurt or rejected. I also understand the satisfaction in putting all of your faith into something and never being disappointed by it. That "something" is God.

The Bible declares that God is not a man that He should lie and this is encouraging because whether intentional or not, man can lie and disappoint, but God will never do either. After someone breaks our trust, we tend to build a wall that is nearly impossible for anyone to break through. We miss out on wonderful opportunities, relationships, and friendships because we are too afraid of being hurt again.

Let's practice trusting more by putting our faith solely in God. Sheri Rose Shepherd stated it well: The best way to protect yourself from allowing betrayal to extinguish your faith is to put your faith solely in the One who will never betray you. That's Jesus.

With Jesus as your guide you can seek Him for guidance (He never fails), you can seek Him for clarity about situations (He never fails) and you can seek Him for discernment about people and opportunities (He never fails). When you discipline yourself to build your trust in the Lord, you are also conditioning yourself to trust others more. A closer relationship with Christ will help you so much more as you travel life's daily journey. Christ will protect you from danger and speak to you about your situation so that you can make better decisions. Don't allow man, who is imperfect; to discourage you from a trusting relationship with someone who is guaranteed to never let you down.

Trust God with your entire life, your family, your heart. God is trustworthy!

Let any walls down that you've built to protect yourself from hurt or deception and trust God fully in everything you do and with everything you have.

Day 11: Get Moving!

* • * • ● ● ● • * • •

*I do not count myself to have apprehended; but one thing I do,
forgetting those things which are behind and reaching forward to
those things which are ahead, I press toward the goal for the prize of
the upward call of God in Christ Jesus. -Philippians 3:13-14*

Today is one of my favorite days because we will
focus on the future! I'm sure that we've all heard the
saying, "Keep your eyes on the prize." Well that pretty
much sums up the entire scripture for today. No matter
what has happened in life, it is behind you and God has
a purpose for your future. Keep your eyes on that
purpose and do not be distracted by anything else but
the prize, which is eternity with God in Christ Jesus.

Now of course discipleship and heaven are our ultimate eternal goals, but the wonderful thing about God is that He also has earthly "prizes" prepared for us once we achieve our "earthly" goals. God has placed desires in us to be fulfilled here on earth that we will use for His Glory. Those are the desires of our hearts that are talked about in Psalm 37:4.

When God formed us, He already knew everything there was to know about us. He knew what we would like, what we would be, and of course He knew the plan He had for us. Our job is to seek Him for guidance on how to fulfill that plan, but also to realize that achieving our goals takes determination. The beautiful thing about God is that He does not throw us to the wolves to figure out our purpose on our own. All we have to do is communicate with Him and He will lead us directly to our desired destination.

As the scripture indicates, there will be obstacles and stumbling blocks along our journey in life. Times will get tough; we will get distracted or even thrown off course, but through it all we have to continue on the journey to our destination. That's the key message of today's scripture—tenacity. You cannot give up on your goals or become distracted simply because the journey was more than you expected.

One thing that stands out to me about this scripture is the line that says, "forgetting those things which are behind and reaching forward to the things that are ahead." We discussed this a tad bit when we talked about forgiveness; the past will only hold you back, you have to move forward! As I mentioned earlier, "keep your eyes on the prize" and let nothing deter you from your destiny.

Today we have a bit of homework. If you have never done so, I would like to encourage you to develop a vision board. Many people create their vision boards at the start of the new year; but the truth is, anyone can have a new beginning at any time of the year. Start off your new beginning by writing your goals and vision for this year. Think about how you will achieve your goals and also think about possible barriers or stumbling blocks that will try to get in your way.

This will be the strategy for achieving your goals. By writing the goals down, thinking about possible stumbling blocks and also thinking about ways to overcome those stumbling blocks, you will already be one step closer to your desired outcome. I'd like to advise you to become less discouraged and more strategic. The blessing in all of this is that you don't even have to develop the strategy; God will give it to you.

Today remember, keep pressing and keep moving; let nothing stop you from the destiny that God has custom designed just for you.

Day 12: Thank God for Grace!

* * * * * ● ● ● * * * *

And if by grace, then it cannot be based on works; if it were,
grace would no longer be grace -Romans 11:6

Webster's dictionary defines grace as "unmerited divine assistance given to humans for their sanctification" or as "a virtue coming from God." I want you to first understand that grace by definition alone is unmerited. This means that we are not deserving of God's grace. The second thing to understand is that it is *given* to us. You cannot earn something that is given. Because of His love for us, God freely gives us grace, which is in no way based on anything that we do or don't do.

Today let's look at grace as it pertains to suffering. You may think the more you suffer, the more grace is given; or the more you bear, the greater the grace. Neither is the case. Grace doesn't depend on suffering to exist, but where there is suffering, there is grace. In the midst of our pain, God can give us grace. When we come to Him confessing our sins, God can give us grace through His mercy and forgiveness. Remember that when you are going through something, God's favor is upon you and can bring you out of it.

If you look at the passage from Romans, you can begin to think differently about grace. The passage states that if grace were based on works—things that we do—then it would no longer be grace. God wants us to know that He is gracious and forgiving to us even though we are unworthy. That should make you want to

Rejoice! God is saying to us, No matter what you do, I am here. If you fall short (which we all do) I will be here. He is letting us know that He is unchanging. What are you going through in your life? Whatever it is, know that God's hand is on you. Pray and draw closer to Him. Have faith in His power to take care of your situation. We only have to have faith, especially during the hard times, to know that God's grace is sufficient to bring us through anything.

Day 13: Staying Focused! (Eyes)

* * * * * ● ● * * * *

Turn my eyes away from worthless things; preserve my life

according to your Word. - Psalm 119:37

How many of us have been told not to do something by our parents, but ignored their words of wisdom? The consequences of disobeying them were probably not good. You may have found out that you should've listened to them and avoided the situation altogether. Instead of a warning from our earthly parents, today's scripture is a statement from the Holy Bible telling us to turn away from things that have no value so that we may live our lives according to God's Word.

We've all heard the statement "look but don't touch." I don't know about you, but for me sometimes it's harder not to touch after I've looked. It's easier for me to resist the urge to buy a new dress that I can't afford if I just stay out of the mall. The scripture tells us to turn our eyes away from valueless things and the best way to ensure that we do this is to never look in the first place. Sometimes we set ourselves up to be trapped by submitting to the "look but don't touch" mentality of this world. We needn't worry about being trapped if we simply learn to avoid the traps altogether.

How do we avoid these traps in a world that is designed to shift our awareness away from God's plan for us? The answer is simple: by immersing ourselves in the Word of God. The second part of this scripture talks about preserving our lives according to His Word. The

STEPHANIE C. LEWIS

word preserve means to safeguard or maintain. The only way to make certain that we don't engage in the foolishness of this world is to read the Bible and pray God's Word over our lives. The scripture is not just meant to be a daily read that you check off on your to-do list, but it is meant to be used as a protective guide so you can concentrate on the calling that God has put on your life.

Our attention can be easily captured by what goes on at work, on social media, television or even in our own neighborhoods. The lives and possessions of others can seem so attractive to us, but can I tell you, everything that is attractive in this world is not of God. We must be able to decipher what is God's will for us and turn away from anything that is not. So when you pray, do so expectantly. Ask God for wisdom to know

63

what is good for you. When you pray in this way, hopeful that God has a purpose for you, then you can be assured that He will answer you.

Day 14: The Power of Vision

* * * * * ● ● * * * *

Then the LORD replied: "Write down the revelation and make it plain on tablets so that a herald may run with it. For the revelation awaits an appointed time; it speaks of the end and will not prove false. Though it lingers, wait for it; it will certainly come and will not delay. - Habakkuk 2:2-3

Throughout the Bible there are stories in which God has put a vision in someone's life and it came to pass. Abraham and Sarah wanted a child and even though both of them were old and it seemed impossible, God brought that vision to life. David, the youngest son, was promised that he would have a mighty Kingdom. God not only brought that vision to life, but God made his kingdom continue on forever. What is the vision that God has given you and what are you doing to fulfill it?

I want to tell you that vision without action is just a dream! Action without vision wastes time! Vision + Action = Change the World. Do you understand that, my sister? Without putting work into your vision it is just a dream, destined to die and not come to pass. Making a dream into a vision requires work! David did not just sit around and twiddle his thumbs, he went out and fought in armies. He had to slay giants in order to get where God wanted him to be. There are some giants in your life that you have to slay. Don't be afraid, because with God on your side you can do it!

Action without vision passes time. More importantly action without vision wastes time. Do you recall that Abraham and Sarah tried to have a baby on their own without God? Even though God promised them a son, they gave up because they looked at their circumstances. Sarah convinced Abraham to make a baby with their servant and that opened up a can of worms! That plan didn't work because it wasn't a part of God's plan for them! But trust me, God will make it work, even with the unneeded assistance He received from you. If we act without considering God's vision for us, we will surely waste our time and energy. You will find that when you try to do things your way they just won't work out.

If we align our vision and action together we can bring change. I'm not talking about small change: pennies and nickels. I'm talking about *big* change. Change that can impact millions of people. Vision + Action = Change the World. Aligning our vision and actions together means that we are taking God's plan for our life and matching it with the things that God is telling us to do. It means that we are basking in God's goodness and really doing everything He asks of us. This step requires faith because we may not always understand what God is doing, but if we hold on, we move closer to our dream. If we will just be obedient, we will find that everything God is asking us to do has purpose.

Habakkuk tells us to write down our revelations, make them plain. Write down your vision, pray over it and then ask God to connect you with the actions to bring it to life. Match up your vision and your actions and you'll be unstoppable. With God on your side, your vision and actions working together will indeed Change. The. World.

Day 15: It's Not About You!

* * * * ● ● ● * * * *

Do nothing out of selfish ambition or vain conceit, but in humility consider others better than myself. -Philippians 2:3

What would have happened to us if Christ had decided that He'd rather spare His flesh than be persecuted and slain at the cross? The world would be lost. We would have no one to intercede on our behalf. Christ came to this earth as the physical embodiment of God and even though He knew what would happen to Him, He fulfilled His end of the bargain, knowing that His pain and sacrifice was for a greater cause. Christ, who was blameless and without sin, was willing to humble Himself and be presented as a living sacrifice;

we who are imperfect and born of sin should be willing to do the same.

The Bible is filled with examples of the humility and selfless acts of Christ. He made himself a servant to mankind and in doing so gave us a perfect depiction of how we should live our lives. As Christians we must understand that God's plan is bigger than our lives; it's bigger than anything we could ever dream of. And guess what? It doesn't just involve us! 2 Peter 3:9 says "it is the will of God that no one shall perish." That means that God wants each and every one of us to repent and come to Him. God wants to save others and He wants to do it through us.

Overcoming the obstacles of life is not only meant for our benefit. When we have gone through something and come out on the other side it propels us forward, but it also acts as a testimony of the goodness and mercy of God. We are to share those times so that those who are going through something similar have hope that what God has done for us can be manifested in their lives too. When we hold back our testimonies, we rob God of His glory and the chance to bring another struggling soul to the Kingdom.

What I want to impart to you today is that God wants us to be generous. He wants us to put others first. Even in the midst of our trials we can focus on others. There is always someone who is worse off than we are. What is not enough for us is more than enough for someone else. We need not worry about ourselves because God has promised to take care of us and the more He has blessed us with, the more generous He expects us to be.

This idea of generosity also extends to our gifts and talents. The Bible speaks plainly about our spiritual gifts and how they should be used for the common good. We shouldn't horde our abilities, picking and choosing who we share them with. They are meant for the "common good," that means for everyone's benefit. That lovely voice you have, but only use in the shower or in your car on the way to work is meant to be shared with others so they too may know God.

That charismatic leadership ability you have should not be wasted at the lunch table, drawing others into a gossip conversation about your boss and coworkers. Instead it should be used to tell someone about Christ and invite them to a place of worship. Let today be the day when you commit to following Jesus' example of selflessness, knowing that what God has blessed you to

bless others and edify His Kingdom.

Day 16: Testing Cultural Toxins

•   •   •   •   ●   ●   ●   •   •   •   •

But examine everything carefully; hold fast to that which is good;
abstain from every form of evil. -1 Thessalonians 5:21

Americans usually have two times a year when they really clean: Just before New Year's Day and again in the spring. We clean before New Year's Day because we want to make sure that our house is clean going into a new year. Spring cleaning means that we get into all of the cracks and crevices when leaning things that we haven't cleaned all year. During this time we may clean baseboards, ceiling fans, or make a pile of things to give away to family or local charities. During both instances we are purging, getting rid of unwanted or toxic things.

Today's scripture asks you to do the same with your life. When was the last time you examined your life to see if you have any toxic people or circumstances on board? Before we move on let's define what toxic is. It's not someone or something that you don't like, makes you uncomfortable or proves to be difficult. So please don't go and remove complex people and things from your life just because they are challenging.

Toxic things and people are poisonous to you; they are deadly; they have the ability to cut you off from God's blessings. In your quest to stay away from or purge these people/things from your life, you have to ask yourself three things: 1) Am I being entertained by sin?   2) Is this pleasing to God?   3) Does this lure me away from Christ?

Am I entertaining sin?   When we wonder if something should be considered sin, we usually compare it to the ten commandments.   Honor thy mother and thy father. *Check.* Thou shall not steal. *Check.*   Don't murder or have false gods. *Check* and *check.*   When Jesus came to earth; however, He gave us a new commandment "to love one another" (John 13:34).

Everything that Jesus did was based on love. If we are not abiding in love, then we are abiding in sin. Being entertained by gossip, being hateful and unforgiving, all of those things are sinful. If we are being around people who behave in such a way or who are encouraging us to live a sinful life, we must separate ourselves. We can only remain in those situations if we are being a Godly influence on them, but the minute they become an influence on us, we must make the decision to part ways.

Is this pleasing to God? This is a question that we have to ask ourselves in private. No one but God knows every single thing we do. In everything we do, especially those done in private, we must ask ourselves if God would be pleased by our actions. If the answer is no, then we must stop. Sometimes it's not easy to stop these things. Sometimes we have strongholds that attach themselves in the form of bad habits and addictions. Know that God has given us the "power to demolish strongholds" (2 Corinthians 10:4). By using God's divine weapons, we can break down anything that has us in bondage. We need only to keep praying and seeking Him to do so.

Does this lure me away from Christ? The final question I want you to focus on today is perhaps the most important one. Are these people, situations, or things luring you away from Christ? Do you find that the more you hang out with these people or the more you indulge in this thing, the further away from Christ you seem to be? If you've stopped seeking God because of people or things that is a red flag and means you may need to do some purging. Start to examine the people and circumstances in your life. Enlist the help of God by asking Him to guide you in this way. In order for you to move to the next level, you must get rid of the things that are holding you down. It's time to clean house.

Day 17: True Beauty

* * * ● ● ● ● ● ● ● ●

Your beauty should not come from outward adornment, such as elaborate hairstyles and the wearing of gold jewelry or fine clothes. Rather, it should be that of your inner self, the unfading beauty of a gentle and quiet spirit, which is of great worth in God's sight.
-1 Peter 3:3-4 (NIV)

Ladies, we are bombarded by images that show us "beauty." To some, beauty is full lips, hips or long hair. To others it's make-up and plastic surgery. In many cases the higher the heels, the more attractive the legs. And let's not even begin to mention what we pluck, shave, tweeze or wax (none of which sounds remotely comfortable) so our appearance mirrors that of acceptance. The beauty industry (hair, make-up, plastic surgery) is a trillion-dollar business. We spend so much time and money on things that in the end are not a determination of true beauty.

The Bible tells us that our beauty doesn't come from outer appearance but from our inner spirit. I'm not telling you to neglect your outer appearance. If we look at the example of Queen Esther in the Bible, we will see a woman who took great care to make herself presentable. She went through a year-long beautification process to prepare herself for the king. In the end she did become queen and savior of her people. However it isn't Esther's beauty alone that makes her such a wonderful example. She was also wise and put others before herself. She was beautiful on the inside and out.

As a woman I understand the desire to do things that enhance your own beauty, even if those things are uncomfortable. I also know that just like a fading, superficial beauty will not last, if all you have going for you is your outward appearance, you may get to some places, but you will never get to where God wants you to be. If you're banking on your physical attractiveness as your ticket to success, just know that outward beauty fades. There is no guarantee that you will always look the way you do or have the income to buy expensive clothes jewelry or make-up. What you will always have is your inner beauty. That cannot be taken away by age, the loss of income or an accident.

God wants us to take care of ourselves in every way. That means giving attention to our outer appearance. More importantly, though, it means making sure that we have a gentle spirit, that we show our Christ-like love in everything we do. Our beauty should be seen by blind men, because we bear good fruit that cannot be observed through regular sight. Today please know that splendor isn't just good looks and fancy clothes; it's letting what God has put on the inside of you come out.

Day 18:

Seeking & Knowing God

● ● ● ● ● ● ● ● ● ● ●

...if you will receive my words and treasure my commandments within you, make your ear attentive to wisdom, incline your heart to understanding; For if you cry for discernment, lift your voice for understanding; If you seek her as silver and search for her as for hidden treasures; then you will discern the fear of the LORD and discover the knowledge of God. –Proverbs 2:1-5 (NASB)

We all have a relationship with someone or something. We have relationships with our spouse, children, parents, friends, co-workers and even our pets. Each relationship is different; but if it is meaningful, the odds are that it took some time and effort to get it that way. God wants to have a meaningful relationship with us. He doesn't want us to have a Sunday-only prayer or only at mealtime/bedtime, or Lord, I need you right now, kind of relationship. He wants our all, because he knows that having that deep relationship with Him will help us in every aspect of life.

God is our Heavenly Father who cares for us infinitely more than even our earthly parents can. He knew us before we were formed in our mothers' womb and wants us to have a life of abundance here on earth. We can only begin to tap into what God has for us by spending time with Him. That time isn't going to come by just wishing. It's only going to come through deliberate action and hard work. It may be hard to squeeze in time with God, but the truth is we make time for things that are important to us. I'm here to tell you that God is important and it is time that we demonstrate our love for and obedience to Him by showing up.

Having a relationship with God means that you have access to a power that is unmatched by anything else. Today's scripture uses words such as "seek," "cry," and "make." These words imply that having a relationship with God requires some work on our part. The scripture also uses the word "receive." After we have put in the work to build that relationship with God, we will receive wisdom, discernment, knowledge and understanding. This can only be accomplished through knowing God on a personal level and reading His Word.

Developing your relationship with God doesn't have to equate to hours on your knees in the prayer closet (though sometimes this may be called for). It does require you to set aside some time. At first it may be 5 or 10 minutes when you wake up in the morning. During that time thank God for what He's doing or has already done in your life. You may want to find a Bible verse to help you through a particular situation. The important thing here is to start setting aside time so that it becomes a daily and habitual thing. Soon you'll find that you are talking with God throughout the day and spending more quiet time with Him. You will then start to see how God brings understanding to your life and gives you power to conquer anything you may face.

Day 19: What Are You Hearing? (Ears)

• • • • • ● ● • • • •

*Consequently, **faith comes** from **hearing** the message, and the message is heard through the word about Christ. – Romans 10:17*

Have you ever seen children cover their ears and shout "I can't hear you!"? This may have evoked images of you as a child or your own children behaving in this way. I think that children have it right. Sometimes we must cover our ears to drown out the noise of life so that we can hear from God. There is a direct connection between what you hear and what you believe. Guard your eyes, ears, and heart with an electric fence. Hear, receive and respond.

Hear only the word of God. We know that almost everything in the world today is in direct contradiction to the Word of God. The news tells us to worry about the state of the economy, terrorists, job security, our children's education. Although those are important issues, we only have to look in the book of Matthew to find passages that tell us *not* to worry. So why are we entertaining anything other than what God has already written and worked out for us?

The answer is that we are receiving all the messages that we hear, but many of those messages do not align with God's Word. Examine the music that you listen to, the television shows that you watch, even some of the people that you listen to. Everything you allow to flow into your space has an impact on you, and yet it is not all meant to do you any good. All of those things are distractions designed by the enemy so that you lose your focus. You believe the media hype or the words of others because you haven't been empowered by the Word to believe otherwise.

The enemy knows that if you focus on the Word of God your ears become a filter for the truth. The Word tells us how to live and assures us of the plan God has for us. Though the Bible was written thousands of years ago, it is still the most relevant book in the world. You have only to look at how many copies have been sold to confirm this. Therefore, you must make it a priority to hear the Word, receive it and respond to it by applying it to your life.

Day 20: What Are You Thinking About? (Mind)

Finally, brothers and sisters, whatever is true, whatever is noble, whatever is right, whatever is pure, whatever is lovely, whatever is admirable—if anything is excellent or praiseworthy—think about such things. -Philippians 4:8

Paul wrote to the Philippians from prison. He had already determined to not think about his circumstances, but to think positively about his situation. Whatever you are thinking about, if it does not align with the Word, cast it away. There is a relationship between your thoughts and everything else in your life. I've summed up that relationship with the following quote: Watch your thoughts, they become your words. Watch your words, they become your actions. Watch your actions, they become your habits. Watch your habits, they become your character. Watch your character, for it becomes your destiny.

Watch your thoughts, they become your words. I'm sure you can think of a time when your thoughts led you to say something that you later regretted. When you allow yourself to meditate on negative things, you will ultimately start to speak in the same manner. The issue is not that we actually have those thoughts, but that we allow those thoughts to formulate into words. The Bible tells us in 2 Corinthians 10:5 to "take captive every thought to make it obedient to Christ." If our thoughts do not align with the Word of God, then we must quickly dismiss them so we don't speak out loud anything that could be harmful to ourselves or to others.

Watch your words, they become your actions. The reason why it's so important to guard your thoughts is that they are a precursor to words that in turn determine our actions. There are so many stories about millionaires who confessed their success out loud before they saw any increase in their earnings. Speaking those words of affirmation remind us of the actions we need to take to obtain those goals. Similarly if your words are harmful or discouraging, you are setting yourself up for your actions to follow suit. There is a reason the Bible tells us the power of life and death is in the tongue (Proverbs 18:21). Words have the power to stop us from pursuing our purpose or can propel our actions toward accomplishing our dreams.

Watch your actions, they become your habits. Action is a noun that means the act of doing something. When we do something over and over again, it becomes a habit. Our actions can help us form good or bad habits. If our thoughts produce words that are good and those words produce positive actions, then we will in turn develop good habits. In the same fashion bad thoughts give way to negative words and actions that can open the door for corruptible habits.

Not one person on earth has a habit that did not formulate from a thought. A person who smokes cigarettes had to first think about it, convince themselves to try it (speak words), actually try it (action) and then do it over and over again to become addicted (habit). If you want to have good habits, ones that are helpful, you must do the right things over and over again. This takes commitment and the mindset that Paul talks about in our scripture for today. Forming a habit takes dedication and will call for you to focus on the noble, admirable and praiseworthy things in order to keep going.

Watch your habits, they become your character. Your habits help shape you as a person. They are the customs that determine everything from how you live to your sleep patterns and even how you eat. Each and every one of your habits come together to form your character. Your personality is revealed to the world every time you interact with others. When you make it a habit to watch your thoughts, words and actions, you allow yourself to develop good character.

Watch your character, it becomes your legacy. Legacy is what you leave behind as an inheritance. It's not always the physical things that you leave behind, rather it's the impact you have had as a person. Your character, who you are, is very important because it *is* your legacy. What will the world, or those you have touched during your lifetime, say about you? It will all depend on how you first chose to *think.* Go all the way back to the beginning of today's message and you will find that your character, your legacy both hinge on how you chose to think about everything. First watch your thoughts, because they will ultimately determine your words, actions, habits, character and yes, your legacy. I urge you to guard them well and take Paul's advice and focus on what is *true, noble, right, pure, lovely, admirable, excellent and praiseworthy.* Think on those things.

Day 21: Just Let Them Do It!

* * * * ● ● ● * * * *

Bless those who curse you, pray for those who mistreat you.

-Luke 6:28

On my way to the airport, a car decided to force its way in front of us. I told my friend to just let him do it, because we weren't trying to get into any accidents. At that point I stated, "Sometimes you just gotta let them do it, girl!" My friend turned to me and said, "Hey that's a good blog title!" I thought about it for a minute, and she was right. With the right perspective you can see a lesson in everything. The lesson in this is, you can't always control everyone or everything. Sometimes you just have to let stuff or people happen. I guess you need some specifics, huh? Well I would be happy to help.

You have a coworker who is hard to deal with. You have done everything in your power to fix the situation, including being difficult yourself, talking to your supervisor and actually confronting the person. I know it's hard to accept, but sometimes you just have to let people be who they are, and you be who you are.

When I say you be who you are, I don't mean the fleshly you. I mean the Christian you. Continue to be respectful and kind to the person. Pray for them and yourself too. You have to pray that you respond the way Christ wants you to and not the way you (your flesh) wants you to respond. If you can't find the lesson yourself, pray for God to show it to you. You will be amazed how God will look out for you and change the situation.

I really don't think I have to give another example. You can use the situation above in many ways. Maybe it's not at work, but at home, school, or just in the passing of the day. Sometimes we can let people or situations change us. Our moods become sour and as a result we behave in negative ways. I can remember times when something happened to me and I just felt heavy with negative emotions. They can come in the form of stress, anxiety or even a bad attitude. God wants us to stay the same, even when our circumstances or people tempt us to behave in a manner that is not pleasing to Him.

Think of how freeing it is to just give those situations to God. We have to practice letting things go, and not letting them bother us as much. Practice makes perfect. Once you have achieved this, watch how your life changes. Start practicing it today... take a deep breath and just let...it... *go.*

Day 22: When God Says Move, Move!

• • • • ● ● ● • • • •

Whether the cloud stayed over the tabernacle for two days or a month or a year, the Israelites would remain in camp and not set out; but when it lifted, they would set out. ²³ At the Lord's command they encamped, and at the Lord's command they set out. They obeyed the Lord's order, in accordance with his command through Moses.
-Numbers 9:22-23

Today's devotional is simple: When God tells you to do something, just do it! Nike had a campaign that began in the late 1980's. Their campaign was "Just do it!" The company flooded radio and television with ads of sports stars like Michael Jordan, Bo Jackson and Kobe Bryant, showing their ability and telling kids "just do it."

The "it" was anything that you put your mind to. As a result the campaign was extremely successful. If millions of people can be inspired by a company to go out there and just do it, you should be even more motivated to move when God tells you to. He is telling you to move so that you can become a success and live out the calling He has on your life, which is infinitely more wonderful than you could ever imagine.

Don't shy away from God's calling just because you think you aren't able to do what He's asking. It doesn't matter if you don't feel like you are what God says you are. It's not about what you feel, it's about what He says you can do. Don't ignore God's message to move because He will always equip you to do what He is asking. Trust me, He wouldn't be telling you to do it, If He didn't feel like it was for you.

I am finally doing exactly what God has put in my heart all these years. I'm on my new journey as an author. That's right, I'm writing a book for you Wonderful Princesses. I was quite nervous when God told me to write this devotional, but I trust Him completely. And now I'm so excited to be going on this journey with you!

What is God telling you to do? Don't add any unnecessary delay to your purpose. The enemy will try to do that enough without your help. But don't let that scare you. You got this, Princess; I believe in you!! Furthermore God, our Heavenly Father believes in you! God has said it, so let's *move*!

Day 23: It's Just A Bad Day, Not A Bad Life

• • • • • ● • • • • •

Count it all joy, my brothers, when you meet trials of various kinds, for you know that the testing of your faith produces steadfastness. And let steadfastness have its full effect, that you may be perfect and complete, lacking in nothing.
-James 1:2-4

Don't you know that a bad day can give you a poor outlook on life? Ask a person how their life is going on a good day and they will tell you about their many blessings and how God is working in their lives. Catch them on a bad day and the same person may tell you about everything that is *not* a blessing. All of a sudden because of their circumstances they aren't as blessed, even though they still have the same things they had on a good day; it's just that their circumstances may have changed a little.

I can think back to a day when I allowed events to taint my outlook on life. It was a Friday and I was heading to the airport for weekend travel. I was upset when the shuttle dropped me off on the wrong side of the airport, making my walk a bit longer than usual. I rushed into the airport, lost my license in the process, and found out that my flight was delayed for 2 1/2 hours. I went on a trek to find my license but was unable to, but I just happened to have my work ID and a bill in my purse, which I was able to use for verification.

When I checked in I found out that my flight was actually delayed for 3 hours. Well, 3 hours turned into 4. I decided to change my flight to an airline that I was more familiar with, only to find out that the flight was delayed for 45 minutes on that airline too! I was so frustrated that I started to cry!

I didn't know if it was the enemy or God testing me. After praying very hard, I finally reached my destination six hours later. One of my close friends called my experience an adventure. And now that I look back, it actually was an adventure. Who knows why my flight was delayed or why I had to jump through hoops that day. Maybe God saved me from some catastrophic ordeal. I don't have an answer for the why, but I did learn that day that I needed to change my perspective.

My adventure caused me to pray a lot and showed me my lack of trust in God. We all have days when it seems like everything is going wrong; however, we just need to look at things a little differently. In order to change our response, we need to look at every day as a blessing because God chose to wake us up. Every time we are given the opportunity to live another day is a day that we can start anew. It's a day that gives us an opportunity to deepen our relationship with Christ.

That way when things go wrong, we are able to look at them as just another mountain to climb, or another hurdle to jump. Bad days don't last forever... they're just a part of life. Everyone will have them, but it's knowing that they won't last that will help us change our perspective and move us forward.

Day 24: Keep Pressing

I press toward the mark for the prize of the high calling of God in Christ Jesus. -Philippians 3:14 (KJV)

With so many things going on around us we can sometimes let life consume us. Our world is a busy one and if we aren't careful we will get so busy that we start to lose focus. We have to learn to pay attention and keep our eyes on the prize. The enemy wants us to lose sight of what God has for us. He wants us to be afraid to go forward, but today we will learn that it's during the times we feel most afraid that we should remain the most focused.

When we move in the direction God wants us to go, it scares the devil. Let me make one thing clear today: *We. Should.* Scare. *him.* He should be the one afraid, because he knows that when we are walking in God's purpose, his days are numbered. You shouldn't be the one filled with fear, because God's promises, when fulfilled, will bring you nothing but awesomeness.

As I was driving to work one morning I was focused on a scripture from Psalm 91:4 that said: "He will cover you with His feathers, and under His wings you will find refuge; His faithfulness will be your shield and rampart." That awesome scripture means that we need not be afraid because God will cover us. The scripture uses a feather to describe how God will cover us: gently and softly. We will be safe if only we continue on the path that God has for us.

I'm writing to you from personal experience. I know what it means to lose focus and I know what it feels like to get it back. I lost my focus for a while. I didn't know if my writing was making any kind of impact on my readers. I realized, though, that if I didn't write, then I had no chance of making an impact. I knew I had to continue, so I got back to the business that God called me to. I began to write again ... for you ... for me ... for God.

No matter what is happening with you or around you, you must keep going. Keep praying. Keep seeking. *Don't Lose Focus!* God loves you and He needs you. He has a purpose and a place for you. Meditate on the scriptures today and let them lead you on your quest to regain focus.

Day 25: What Does Your "Yes" Look Like?

For I know the plans I have for you," declares the LORD, "plans to prosper you and not to harm you, plans to give you hope and a future. -Jeremiah 29:11

God has a plan for you. Yes, you. He hasn't thrown you away because of your mistakes and your past. He hasn't written you off because you have been disobedient. He has had a plan for you since before you were born and nothing you say or do will change that fact. When you don't have a plan, God does. Even if you have your own plan for your life, just know that God's plan is infinitely greater than yours and serves a purpose higher than we could ever understand. God just wants you to say yes to the plan He has for your life.

Saying yes to God can be both scary and exciting, but ultimately it will be rewarding. Sometimes God calls us to do things that have us thinking, "You have the wrong person, God. That's not me." Oh, but it is you, my sister. And just because you can't see it, doesn't mean it's not true.

We tend to think we aren't good enough, strong enough, smart enough. I'll tell you a little secret: God already knows what you are capable of. It's time for you to learn what you are capable of. You do what you can do and God will always make up the rest by doing everything we can't.

When God says Yes, that means you are qualified. We only have to look at some of the people He uses in the Bible to understand this concept. In the Bible God uses Moses (a person with a speech impediment), Zacchaeus (an unpopular man who hung out in trees) and Mary Magdalene (an afflicted and hurt woman). Though these are just a few people who were used by God, they were placed in those positions to show us that God uses those who people least expect. Why? Because He wants to show us we don't have to be qualified in the eyes of the world, or even qualified in our own eyes to do His work.

Just like the people in the Bible, we have to be totally dependent on God to lead us in our journey. We have to be assured that His plan is what's best for us and for His Kingdom.

Never be afraid to say yes to God's plans because you think you're unqualified. You are a vessel God wants to use for the building up of His Kingdom. Trust Him! When you fulfill God's plan for you, you can humble yourself and give Him the glory for helping you.

Think about what God is asking you to do. To those of you who have clarity in this matter, step out and watch how God miraculously strategizes to move you forward. For those of you who aren't sure, ask Him, but I have a feeling you know; you just need a little more confirmation. I hope you count today's devotional as confirmation, because it is. It's Time To Say Yes!

Day 26: The Spirit Perspective

Consider the blameless, observe the upright; a future awaits those who seek peace. -Psalm 37:37

A worldly perspective always leaves us wanting more. I had a picture with a caption that said "Once everything falls into place, I will find peace." Let me tell you right now there will never be a time when everything just "falls into place."

Though you are a Princess in the eyes of God, the world is not equipped with fairy godmothers who wave their wands and magically make all of our issues go away. Not even our Heavenly Father will make *all* our issues disappear. They exist to make us into the people God wants us to be. Even though there will never be that perfect moment, it doesn't mean we cannot live in perfect peace.

The scripture tells us a future waits for those who "seek" peace. This means that just like we pursue an appointment at the nail shop when we need a manicure, we must pursue peace. Sometimes we can automatically conjure peace, other times we must actively engage in peace. Job 3:26 reads "I have no peace, no quietness; I have no rest, but only turmoil."

Even Job, a man who was upright in the eyes of God had moments when his perspective was skewed. He was being mercilessly attacked by the devil and at that moment he had no peace. I don't know about you, but that is not the life I want to live.

Even in the midst of his suffering Job relied on God and that is what we should do as well. I don't want you to wait around for things to be perfect in order for you to have peace. You can have peace at any time if you look at life from the spirit-led perspective. Your peace is already there, because Jesus left it for us, you just have to access it.

It's like having the electricity turned on and expecting an unplugged lamp to work. You have to plug that lamp into a socket to access the electricity in order for it to turn on. That's how it is with us and God. You have to plug in, to connect with God to access your peace and look at your situation from the spirit perspective. Don't try to perfect your life, thinking peace will come when you have it all together; we need God for that. He wants to give you a great life and a peaceful life. Choose the spirit perspective, because it leads to the peace perspective!

Day 27: Just Say NO!

* * * * ● ● ● * * * *

In the same way, let your light shine before others, that they may see your good deeds and glorify your Father in heaven.
-Matthew 5:16

Woman to woman, sometimes you just have to say "No," and that's perfectly ok! Your light can't shine if you're tired or burnt out from doing everything for everybody else. I'm not telling you not to help; God wants us to do that. There is a difference, though, between being busy doing the Lord's work and just plain being busy. Just being busy bears little to no fruit. Are you ever so busy making things happen that you take a step back and realize you have not gotten very far? Those are the times you must muster up the strength to say no to some things.

Believe me, I know firsthand how pressured you can feel to say yes to the many requests that come your way, especially when it comes to family or close friends. However, if it takes you away from walking in or fulfilling your God-given purpose at that moment, you should probably say no. Everything you do must have purpose. Whether it's taking some much-needed time for yourself or finally working on that business God's been putting in your mind for the last couple years. You have to decide to say no to the people and things that are hindering you from your purpose. If you are not sure if you should say no, here are some questions you can ask yourself to determine the right answer.

1. *Is this going to help me fulfill my purpose? If so, how?* Sometimes connecting your actions to a purpose can help you figure out if you should take on a task. Deliberately linking your actions to your purpose will help weed out some of the duties that have no value.

2. *Am I doing this because God placed it on my heart to do or because I feel guilty or pressured to do it?* Oh it's hard to overcome guilt! We may feel guilty because we can't help someone or because what they are asking us to do just doesn't fit with the plans God has for us. Guilt can hold us back and cause us to accept responsibilities that have nothing to do with us. If you find yourself feeling guilty about making a decision you know is right,

ask God to help you refocus your attention on His plan for you.

3. *If I do this, will it be pleasing to God or will it pull me away from Him?* Not everything that someone asks of us is of God. When you spend time with God, you will know instantly what is pleasing to Him. Stay away from people and activities that will draw you away from God.

If you answer these questions honestly, you will know if you should say yes or no. We have to make sure that we are intentional about our actions. Our intention is to fulfill our God-given purpose. In order to do this, sometimes we have to disappoint our family and friends. I'd rather disappoint friends and family if it keeps me from disappointing God. Saying "No" allows us to get busy doing God's work so that our light will

shine and our good deeds will be known.

Day 28: Time to Release

And no one pours new wine into old wineskins. Otherwise, the wine will burst the skins, and both the wine and the wineskins will be ruined. No, they pour new wine into new wineskins. -Mark 2:22

If you have children, then you know there comes a time when you have to buy new clothes and shoes because they have outgrown them. Even if you don't have kids you can understand the concept of something that doesn't fit anymore. My question to you today is what or who have you outgrown? What is it in your life that doesn't fit? Today I want to focus on why it is important to get rid of old things that just don't work anymore.

Our society seems to think that new is better and to some extent that is true. We need new things in our lives sometimes. God wants to bring us new things. The scripture today talks about pouring new wine into new wineskins. In order for God to give us the new, we have to get rid of the old things that cause ruin in our lives.

That baggage that is weighing us down is actually hindering what God wants to do in our lives. Don't hold on to the things and people of your past that mean you no good. Just like pouring wine into old wineskins will cause the skins to burst and ruin the wine, having baggage in your life leaves no room for blessings and ruins the chances for God to move in your life.

Don't get me wrong, God can move in any environment He deems worthy. But if you are so bogged down with burdensome things and people, you can't even begin to see what He has for you. You may already be aware of some things or people you need to let go of. My advice to you is simply this: *Let Them Go!*

Let go of any and everything that stands in the way of God's promises for you. You can't shove your feet into shoes that no longer fit. Don't try to hang on to people and things that no longer fit what God's trying to do in your life. I know it's hard, but trust me when I say: God is going to replace everything with the best for you. You deserve it!

Day 29: You Are Worthy!

* * * * ● ● ● * * * *

For we are God's handiwork, created in Christ Jesus to do good works, which God prepared in advance for us to do. - Ephesians 2:10

I read a quote by an unknown author on social media. It read "Your value does not decrease based on someone's inability to see your worth." I don't know who wrote it, but I knew I had to share it. This quote could describe anyone, including ourselves. Sometimes it's not about anyone else's inability to see our worth, but our lack of capacity to see our self-worth. Many times we are our own worst critics. We downplay our value and in the process, downplay the real contributions we bring. I'm here to tell you to stop it! Stop it right now!

Your assignment today is to take some time to sit and think about why you think you are not worthy of the life God has for you. I use the word "think" because it's only a thought. It's not a reality. God knows that you're worthy, that's why He has called you. I want you to ponder this, because even though what we think isn't always reality, it can be *our* reality. Our reality prompts us to become fearful. We must ask ourselves why we are afraid? What is it that has us so anxious about stepping out to have the life that God has designed for us?

Think about what negative things you are saying to yourself. Write them down and then tear them up. Mentally picture yourself taking all of those negative things and grinding them in the garbage disposal or throwing them into the garbage. Ask God to help you see yourself as He does. You are not a label, rather you are a child of the King. You are set apart to inherit all the things Jesus had. The time to think of yourself as a Princess set to inherit the Kingdom of God is now. Ephesians 2:10 tells us we are God's handiwork. Everything God makes is admirable and precious. You have to stop your pattern of devaluing yourself. You are of value. You are worthy. God says so!

Day 30: Closure

Anyone you forgive, I also forgive. And what I have forgiven—if there was anything to forgive—I have forgiven in the sight of Christ for your sake. -2 Corinthians 2:10

Sophia A. Nelson, an award winning journalist and author once said, "The most painful goodbyes are the ones that are never spoken and never explained. Forgive. Then let them go." We can all probably relate to the goodbyes that Ms. Nelson is talking about. They are the ones that break our hearts because we wish we could have talked to a person one more time to find out "why?" Those of us who are lucky enough to have had that opportunity may have found closure. Some of us who have never had that opportunity still wonder. If you are one of the ones that still think about it, know that talking to that someone isn't the only way to find closure.

Let me first start out by saying even the "lucky" ones who have had conversations may have found they still don't have closure. This is because closure is not found in that type of experience. Closure comes by you accepting what has happened, deciding to forgive that person—and maybe even yourself—and then moving on.

Closure comes with forgiveness. Many people think that forgiveness is for the offender. They think that it blesses the other person by forgiving them. Forgiveness is not for them, it's for you! You need to forgive in order to move forward with your life. Unforgiveness breeds bitterness and resentment. You will never have a life filled with the promises of God if you hold on to such things.

Never in the Bible does it state that these things bear good fruit. Instead in Galatians 5:22-23 we learn that the fruit of the spirit is love, joy, peace, patience, kindness, goodness, faithfulness, gentleness and self-control. We cannot have those things if we insist on a life of unforgiveness. Stop holding on to the past, wishing that things could have been different. Dwelling on it doesn't change what happened. I know this from experience.

Betrayal can hurt, I know, but we can't get to the place God wants us if we hold on to it. We have to release anything we have against another person in order to move forward. God wants us to be in a place fit for a

Queen or Princess and forgiveness is the pathway to that place. Ms. Nelson also said, "Leave the gift of goodbye." Some people need that gift, and you must be ready to give it to them freely, with no strings attached.

To conclude, I leave you with a quote from an unknown source: "Forgive and Forget what and who has hurt you in the past, but never forget what it has taught you." Use those lessons from life to help push you along and fulfill your purpose.

GET UP!!!

Made in the USA
Columbia, SC
21 February 2020